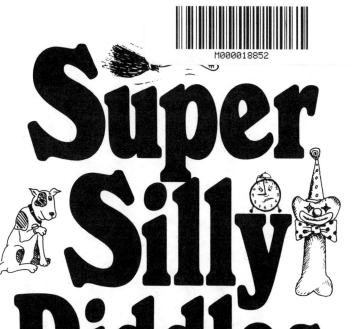

Super Silly Riddles

Gyles Brandreth
Illustrated by John Carter & Jonathan Allen

WINGS BOOKS
New York

This 1991 edition is published by Wings Books,
distributed by Outlet Book Company, Inc., a Random House Company,
225 Park Avenue South, New York, New York 10003, by arrangement
with Sterling Publishing Co., Inc.

Printed and bound in the United States of America

Library of Congress Cataloging-in-Publication Data
Brandreth, Gyles Daubeney, 1948-
    [Big book of silly riddles]
    Super silly riddles / Gyles Brandreth ; illustrated by John Carter
& Jonathan Allen.
        p.   cm.
    Originally published under the title: The big book of silly
riddles.   1987.
    Summary: An illustrated collection of humorous riddles and
puzzles, in such categories as "Crime Does Not Pay," "Absurd
Animals," and "No Laughing in the Library."
    ISBN 0-517-07352-8
    1. Riddles, Juvenile.   [1. Riddles.   2. Puzzles.]   I. Carter,
John, 1930-   ill.   II. Allen, Jonathan, ill.   III. Title.
PN6371.5.B69   1991
828' .91402 — dc20
                                                    91-28855
                                                       CIP
                                                        AC
ISBN 0-517-07352-8
8 7 6 5 4 3 2 1

CONTENTS

· 1 ·
WHAT IS IT?

What can you use for cleaning your teeth, blowing your nose and keeping the rain off?

A toothbrush, a handkerchief and an umbrella, of course!

What is full of holes but holds water?

A sponge.

What did the big red bucket say to the small white bucket?

"You're a little pale (pail)."

What is large enough to hold a pig, but small enough to hold in your hand?
A pen.

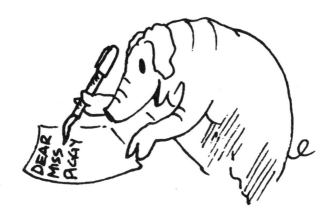

What is the one thing you break as soon as you say its name?
Silence.

What can you break without hitting it or dropping it?
A promise.

What do you lose every time you stand up?
Your lap.

What occurs once in a minute, twice in a moment, but not at all in a split second?
The letter M.

What should you try to keep since nobody else wants to have anything to do with it?
Your temper.

What is always coming, but never arrives?
Tomorrow.

What gets bigger the more you take away from it?
A hole.

What can be right, but never wrong?
A right angle.

What is true to the last?
A shoe.

What makes a pair of shoes?
Two shoes.

What is hard to beat?
A broken drum.

What smells most in a pig sty?
Your nose.

What do you look
into every day?
A mirror.

What is always
down no matter
how high up it
goes?
Goose down.

What is it that you can't hold for half an
hour, even though it's lighter than air?
Your breath.

What do you get if you drop a piano down a
coal mine?
A-flat minor.

What is the difference between a hill and a
pill?
*One is hard to get up, the other is hard to
get down.*

What occurs four times in every week,
twice in every month, but only once in a
year?
The letter E.

What has eyes but cannot see?
A potato.

The person who makes it doesn't need it; the person who buys it doesn't use it for himself; and the person who does use it doesn't know anything about it. What is it?
A coffin.

It burns no coal, no oil, no gas; it doesn't need electricity; and yet it is hotter than an oven, hotter than a fire and even hotter than a furnace. What is it?
The sun.

What falls in winter but never gets hurt?
Snow.

Lucy had it first, Ethel had it last, and David didn't have it at all. Boys never have it, girls have it once, and Miss Sillie had it twice until she married Peter Stupid, and then she never had it again. What is it?

The letter L.

It has no length, no breadth, no thickness, but when someone gives it to you, you can certainly feel it. What is it?

A kiss.

What is it that people always overlook, no matter how careful they are?

Their own noses.

What lives on its own substance, but dies as soon as it devours itself?

A candle.

What is too much for one, enough for two, and nothing at all for three?

A secret.

What is it that nobody wants to have, but nobody would like to lose?

A bald head.

What do you get if you cross an elephant with a boy scout?

An elephant that helps old ladies across the street.

What kind of coat is made without buttons
and is wet when you first put it on?
A coat of paint.

Why is it a good idea to have holes in your
jeans?
So that you can get your legs inside.

What words can be pronounced louder and
quicker by adding a syllable to them?
Loud and quick.

What is the last thing you take off when
you go to bed at night?
Your feet off the floor.

What always goes to bed with shoes on?
A horse.

CAN YOU SAY THESE FIVE TIMES FAST?

Double bubble gum bubbles double.

Cuthbert's custard.

Toy boat.

Miss Ruth's red roof thatch.

Three thrice-freed thieves.

The big black-backed bumble bee.

· 2 ·
FOOD FOR THOUGHT

How do you make gold soup?
You start with fourteen carrots (carats).

What is it that is put on a table, cut and passed, but never eaten?
A deck of cards.

What always stays hot, even it you put it in the refrigerator?
A jar of mustard.

How do you keep flies out of the kitchen?
Put a bucket of manure in the dining room.

What is the simplest way to lose weight?
Get lockjaw.

What should you do if you are hungry but don't want to eat?
Talk to an annoying person until you are fed up.

What did the fat man say when he sat down to eat?
I don't want all this food to go to waist.

How can you recognize rabbit stew?
It has hares in it.

If you were twice as fat as I am, what would you say?
I W (I double you).

What did the meat say when it was about to be put on a skewer?
"Oh, spear me! Spear me!"

What is a doughnut?
Someone who is crazy about money.

Which will burn longer—the candles on a boy's birthday cake or the candles on a girl's birthday cake?
No candles burn longer; they all burn shorter.

Did you hear about the baker who left his job?
He didn't knead the dough.

What kind of beans do cannibals put in their chili?
Human beans (beings).

What did the polar bear have for lunch?
Iceburgers.

If cheese comes on top of a hamburger, what comes after the cheese?
A mouse.

Why should you keep the letter M out of the freezer?
Because it turns ice into mice.

What is musical and handy in a supermarket?
A Chopin (shopping) Liszt.

Do restaurants serve crabs?
Yes, if they sit down.

Which is heavier: a hundred pounds of whipped cream or a hundred pounds of bricks?
They both weigh a hundred pounds.

What's the difference between six dozen dozen eggs, and half a dozen dozen eggs?
Six dozen dozen is 864 and half a dozen dozen is 72, so the difference is 792 eggs.

If it takes three minutes to boil an egg, how long will it take to boil three eggs?
Three minutes. You put them all in the same pot.

Why did the chicken stop in the middle of the street?
She wanted to lay it on the line.

Why did Adam bite the apple?
Because he didn't have a knife.

How does a coffee-pot feel when it's full?
Perky.

How do you make an egg roll?
Push it.

A pilot was flying over the jungle when suddenly he developed engine trouble and was forced to parachute out of the plane. Unfortunately he landed right in the middle of a big pot that a cannibal was cooking. The cannibal was just about to eat his dinner when suddenly he cried: "Wait! What's this flier doing in my soup?"

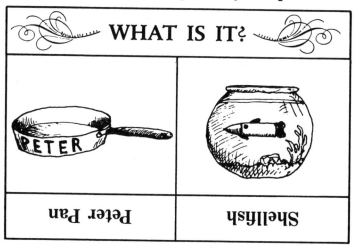

WHAT IS IT?

Peter Pan

Shellfish

What is the best day for making pancakes?
Fryday.

Is it a good idea to eat pancakes on an empty stomach?
No, eat them on a plate.

Is it polite to eat with your fingers?
No, fingers should eat separately.

What did the microwave say to the chef?
"I can make things hot for you."

What makes pies so nosy?
The letter S. It makes spies out of them.

Which two numbers multiplied together
equal 7?
1 and 7.

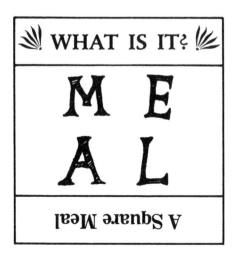

"Shall we have salad?"
"Yes, lettuce!"

What would you call two bananas?
A pair of slippers.

· 3 ·
SICK &
TIRED

What do you call a pony with a sore throat?
A hoarse horse.

Where do you take a sick pony?
To the horsepital.

What is the difference between a tired old horse and a dead bee?
One is a seedy beast; the other is a bee deceased.

Sign outside the vet's office:
HOSPITAL ZONE—NO BARKING.

Why did the cow go to the vet?
Because she was moo-dy.

Why did the cat join the Red Cross?
It wanted to be a first-aid kit.

Why did the shoe go to visit the doctor?
He wanted to get healed (heeled).

Why wasn't Eve afraid of catching measles?
Because she'd Adam.

What has wings, is out of its mind and sits in trees?
A raven lunatic.

What is clean and white and dashes through the desert with a bedpan?
Florence of Arabia.

What kind of doctor treats ducks?
A quack.

If a psychiatrist charged $75 a visit, how much did he charge the elephant for two visits?

$1,150. That's for $150 for two visits, plus $1,000 for two new couches!

What do you give a seasick elephant?
Plenty of room!

What is the best cure for double vision?
Shut one eye.

A famous doctor had a brother who died. The man who died didn't have a brother. So how were the famous doctor and the man who died related?

They were brother and sister. The doctor was a woman.

Name something that runs in families?
Noses, generally.

How long should doctors practice medicine?
Until they get it right.

How can you avoid falling hair?
Jump out of the way.

Why is the letter X like a permanent invalid?
Because it is never in "good health."

What happened to the optician who fell in the lens-grinding machine?
He made a spectacle of himself.

Why was the famous musician struck by lightning?
He was a good conductor.

Why was he arrested?
He got in treble.

Why was he such a great ball player?
He had perfect pitch.

How did he break his leg?
He fell over a clef.

What happened when he died?
He decomposed.

I have five noses, three ears, and one eye.
What am I?
Very ugly.

What is the worst month for soldiers?
A long March.

Why did people tell the dentist to see a
psychiatrist?
He looked down in the mouth.

What did Dracula
say after a visit to
the dentist?
"Fangs a lot."

WHAT ARE THESE PICTURES?

B E D B E D	**K** **C** **E** **H** **C**
Double Bed	Checkup
	↑**SIDE**↓
Pale Face	Upside Down
STAND U **I**	
I Understand You	

· 4 ·
HAVING A
WONDERFUL
TIME

Why are goalkeepers thrifty?
Because saving is their job.

What do you get if you cross a hunting dog
with a telephone?
A golden receiver.

What do you get if you dial 1-853-1013-
76298-0056834?
A sore finger.

What is the difference between a telephone
and a 747?
The 747 is the one without the dial.

What disease do race cars get?
Vroomatism.

What do you have to know to teach an elephant tricks?
More than the elephant.

Did you hear about the wrestler who had to quit his job?
He couldn't get a grip on himself.

Where do butchers dance?
At the meatball.

Where do Easter bunnies dance?
At the basketball.

Where do moon boots dance?
At the football.

What did the football sing to the boot?
"I get a kick out of you."

What did the piece of coal sing to the furnace?
"What kind of fuel am I?"

Who has antlers, white gloves and loves Minnie?
Mickey Moose.

What do librarians do to relax?
They feel a tome (at home).

What is the difference between a basketball and Prince Charles?
One is thrown to the air; the other is heir to the throne.

How do you hold a bat?
By the wings.

What did the rabbits do when they got married?
Went on their bunnymoon.

What is grey, has four legs and a trunk?
A mouse going on vacation.

Where do cows go on vacation?
Moo York.

What do cows do in the city?
Visit the moo-seum (museum).

What did the buffalo say to his son when he went on vacation?
"Bison!"

What do you get if you cross a cow with a camel?

Lumpy milk shakes.

Why are wolves like playing cards?
Because they come in packs.

What is a chicken's favorite movie?
"That's Hentertainment."

Which musical key makes a good army officer?
A-sharp major.

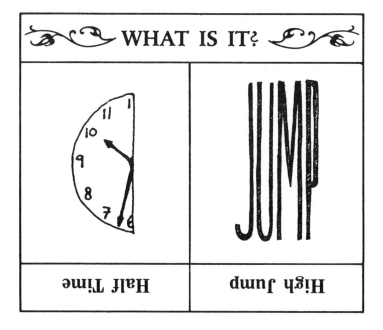

WHAT IS IT?

Half Time

High Jump

Why is the theatre such a sad place?
Because the seats are often in tiers (tears).

Two Canadians went on vacation together. One Canadian is the father of the other Canadian's son. How are the two related?
They are husband and wife.

WHAT ARE THESE PICTURES?

A Masked Ball

Horseshoe

Cookbook

· 5 ·
CRIME DOES NOT PAY

If eight watches were stolen from a jewelry, what criminal would the police look for?

An octopus who is never late.

Can you solve this little puzzle?
> Twice four and twenty blackbirds
> Were sitting in the rain;
> I shot and killed a seventh part—
> How many still remain?

Four (¹⁄₇ of the 28 blackbirds) remain because they are dead. The rest flew away when the gun went off.

Did you hear about the cleaning lady who quit her job?

She found that grime didn't pay.

What goes further the slower it goes?

Money.

Where can you always find money?

In the dictionary.

Why is an empty pocket always the same?

Because there's never any change in it.

Can you divide $4,700 between Tom, Dick and Harry so that Tom gets $1,000 more than Dick, and Dick gets $800 more than Harry?

Tom will get $2,500. Dick will get $1,500 and Harry will get $700.

Why did Robin Hood rob the rich?

Because the poor didn't have any money.

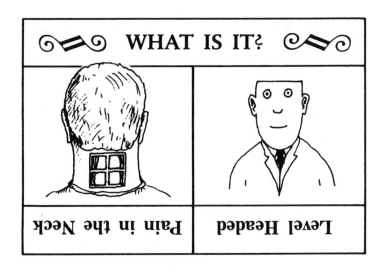

If Fortune had a daughter, what would she be called?
Miss Fortune.

What is the difference between the penniless man and a feather bed?
One is hard up, the other is soft down.

What is the best way to double your money?
Fold it in half.

How can you make a five-dollar bill worth more?
If you fold it, you double it, but if you open it up again, you'll find it increases.

Why did Cain fight with his brother?
Because he was able.

Why should men avoid the letter A?
Because it makes men mean.

What did the thief say when he went to rob the glue factory?
"This is a stick-up."

Why did the prisoner take a ladder into the courtroom?
He wanted to take his case to a higher court.

How did the midget get into the police force?

He lied about his height.

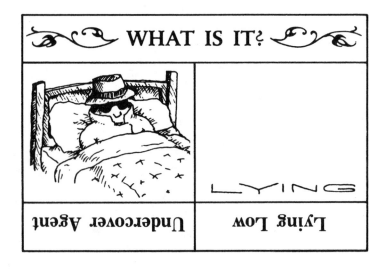

WHAT IS IT?	
	LYING
Undercover Agent	Lying Low

· 6 ·
KEEP IT IN THE FAMILY

Sammy and Sally were born on the same day in the same year and are children of the same parents—and yet they are not twins. How come?

Sammy and Sally are two children from a set of triplets.

My age and that of my daughter are the same with the digits reversed. One year ago I was twice as old as my daughter. How old am I and how old is my daughter?

I am 73 and she is 37.

A man was looking at a painting and said: "Brothers and sisters have I none, but that man's father is my grandfather's son." How is the man related to the man in the painting?

He is looking at a painting of himself!

I have a Russian friend who has three sons. The first son was called Rab and became a lawyer. The second son was called Ymra and became a soldier. The third son has just become a sailor. What do you think he is called?

Yvan, because he joined the navy.

Mr. Bigger got married to Mrs. Bigger in 1969. Who was bigger, Mr. Bigger or Mrs. Bigger?

Mr. Bigger, because he had always been Bigger; Mrs. Bigger hadn't.

In 1970 the Biggers had a little boy and called him Bobby. Who was the biggest then—Mr. Bigger, Mrs. Bigger, or Bobby Bigger?

Bobby, because he is little Bigger.

When Bobby grew up they went to visit him at the university. They had their photograph taken: Mr. Bigger stood next to Mrs. Bigger and Bobby stood on the other side of his mother. Who was the Biggest?

Mrs. Bigger. She was by Father (farther) Bigger.

On one sad day, Mr. Bigger died. It was not long, however, before Mrs. Bigger married Mr. Bigger's brother. So, she was still Mrs. Bigger. Who was the bigger at the wedding, Mrs. Bigger or her new husband?

Mrs. Bigger, because she was twice Bigger.

Mrs. Bigger never stopped loving her first husband even though he was dead. Who was bigger then?

Neither. Mrs. Bigger always said: "This thing is bigger than both of us."

What relation is a doormat to a doorstep?
A step farther.

Why is a baby like an old car?
It never goes anywhere without a rattle.

What is the wife of an engineer called?
Bridget.

What is the wife of a jeweler called?
Ruby.

What did the electrician's wife say when her husband came home late from work?
"Wire you insulate?"

What did the Dutch mother do with her child before dinner?
She washed her Hans.

A boy's father used to collect fleas as a hobby. What did his mother do?
Scratch.

What did the cannibal with a tough father do?
Left him on the side of the plate.

What did the father say to his son who wanted to be a tank driver when he grew up?

"I certainly won't stand in your way."

WHAT IS IT?

Four Crying Out Loud

A man married a widow, and each already had children. Ten years later there was a great battle going on among the twelve children. The mother ran to the father and cried: "Come quickly! Your children and my children are fighting our children!" As the parents now each had nine children of their own, how many had been born during the ten years?

Each had three when they were married. Six have been born since.

Did you hear about the two lighthouse keepers who fell in love?
Their marriage is on the rocks.

Did you hear about the two cheerleaders who got married?
They met by chants.

CAN YOU SAY IT?

Fancy Nancy didn't fancy doing fancy work. But Fancy Nancy's fancy aunty did fancy Fancy Nancy's doing fancy work!

Even Stephen's even oven's on.

Sheila sewed shirts seriously.

The gum glue grew glum.

· 7 ·
ALPHABET SOUP

What letters are most like a Roman emperor?
The C's are (Caesar).

Which letter is like a crazy Roman emperor?
The letter P because it is near O (Nero).

How many peas in a pod?
There is only one P in "pod."

What is pronounced like one letter, written with three letters, and belongs to all animals?
Eye.

When is it correct
to say "I is"?
*"I is the letter
after H."*

How many letters are in the alphabet?
Eleven. T-H-E A-L-P-H-A-B-E-T

Spell extra-wise in two letters.
YY (2 Ys).

What would you say if you opened your
piggy bank and found that there was
nothing inside?
O-I-C-U-R-M-T.

How do you spell blind pig in six letters?
B-L-N-D P-G
(No eyes!).

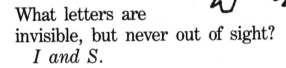

What letters are invisible, but never out of sight?
I and S.

What letter always ends everything?
The letter G.

Why is the letter S a scary letter?
Because it makes cream scream.

What part of London is in France?
The letter N.

What letter has traveled further than any other?
The letter D. It has gone to the end of the world.

What is the longest sentence in the world?
Life imprisonment.

Why are the second and the next-to-last letters of the alphabet so important?
Because we couldn't get BY without them.

What is always in fashion but always out of date?
The letter F.

Spell dry grass in three letters.
HAY.

Why is O the only vowel that is sounded?
Because all the rest are in AUDIBLE.

Why is the letter A like twelve noon?
Because it is in the middle of DAY.

Why is G like the sun?
Because it is in the middle of LIGHT.

Why is the letter K like a pig's tail?
Because it is at the end of pork.

Why is the letter D like a wedding ring?
Because we cannot be wed without it.

What begins with P, ends in E and has thousands of letters in it?
Post Office.

When were there only two vowels?
In the days of No-A and before U and I were born.

Why is a false friend like the letter P?
Because although he's the first in pity, he's always the last in help.

What is the longest word in the English language?
SMILES, because there is a mile between the first and last letters.

Why is the letter A like a flower?
Because a B always comes after it.

Why is the letter T like an island?
Because it is in the middle of water.

What sea has waves but no water?
CBS.

Can you take six away from a king of Israel, and leave his father?
Take VI from DAVID and you get his DAD.

What five-letter word has six left when you take two away?
Sixty.

Make one word from the letters NEW DOOR.
One word.

Why is the letter D like a naughty child?
Because it makes MA MAD.

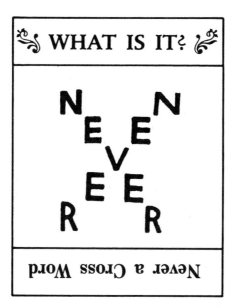

✧ **WHAT IS IT?** ✧

N E E N V E E R R

Never a Cross Word

How many letters are there in the alphabet at Christmas?
Twenty-five, because at Christmas we sing, "No-el."

What letter is never found in the alphabet?
The one you mail.

Which letter of the alphabet would be most useful to a deaf woman?
The letter A, because it would make HER HEAR.

WHAT IS IT?

A Sea Serpent

Why is the letter R important to friends?
Because without it they would be fiends.

What comes after O?
"Yeah!"

When can you spell idiot in one letter?
When it's U!

· 8 ·
WHO'S COUNTING?

A woman who works in a candy store in Boston has measurements 40-26-44, is 5 feet 4 inches tall and wears size 41 shoes. What do you think she weighs?

Sweets.

What is the difference between 100 and 1000?

0.

What do you get if a 350-pound man marries a 250-pound woman?

A big wedding.

If five cats catch five rats in five minutes,
how many cats do you need to catch a
hundred rats in one hundred minutes?
Five.

Why is twice ten like twice eleven?
*Because twice ten is twenty, and twice
eleven is twenty too (two).*

How many times can 100 be subtracted
from 800?
*Only once. After that it isn't 800
anymore!*

What has six legs but only walks with four?

A horse with a rider.

Why do nice, polite people never use the number 288?

Because it is too (two) gross.

If I fainted right now, what number would you bring me?

You would bring me 2.

Can you write down five odd numbers that will add up to 14?

11 + 1 + 1 + 1 = 14

A man gave a party and invited seven people. There were:
- 2 fathers
- 2 mothers
- 1 grandmother
- 3 grandchildren
- 2 sons
- 2 daughters
- 1 brother
- 2 sisters
- 1 father-in-law
- 1 mother-in-law
- 1 daughter-in-law
- 4 children

How come?

There were two sisters and their brother, father, mother and two grandparents.

What odd number—when beheaded— becomes even?

S/even.

What number can you divide in half and have nothing?

8.

If two's company and three's a crowd, what are four and five?

Nine.

When do one and one make more than two?

When they make 11.

When do two and two make more than four?

When you can't add!

〜〜 WHAT IS IT? 〜〜

ONE ANOTHER
ONE ANOTHER
ONE ANOTHER
ONE ANOTHER
ONE ANOTHER
ONE ANOTHER

Six of one, half a dozen of another.

What are arithmetic bugs?
Mosquitoes, because they add to misery, subtract from pleasure, divide your attention and multiply quickly.

If a man was born in the year 50 B.C., how old was he in 50 A.D.?
99 years old. There was no year 0.

I have two coins in my pocket that add up to 55 cents. One of them is not a 50-cent piece. What are the two coins?
One of them isn't a 50-cent piece, but the other is! They are a 50-cent piece and a nickel.

What is the next number in the series 7 9 100 5 7 118 9 0 6?
I have no idea!

What did the adding machine say to the cashier?

"You can count on me!"

CAN YOU SAY IT?

Three free thugs set three thugs free.

Six thick thistle sticks.

Say this sharply, say this sweetly,
Say this shortly, say this softly,
Say this sixteen times in succession.

· 9 ·
ABSURD
ANIMALS

What fish
sings songs?
  *A tuna
  fish.*

What part of
a fish weighs
the most?
  Its scales.

What is a prickly pear?
  Two porcupines (a prickly pair).

Why do squirrels spend so much time in
trees?
  *To keep away from the nuts on the
  ground.*

Did you hear about the frog that parked
his car illegally?
  It got toad away.

Where does a frog change its clothes?
  In a croakroom.

How many sexes are there?
  *Three. The male sex, the female sex and
  insects.*

What is the difference between a coyote and a flea?

One howls on the prairie, and the other prowls on the hairy.

What is the difference between a dog and a flea?

A dog can have fleas, but a flea can't have dogs.

How do you start a flea race?

One, two, flea, go!

How would a skunk smell without a nose?

With a nose or without a nose, he'd still smell terrible.

Why is it hard to talk with a goat around?

Because it always butts in.

What is the difference between a counterfeit bill and a crazy rabbit?
One is bad money, the other is a mad bunny.

What animal do you look like when you take a bath?
A little bear.

What animal can't you turn your back on?
A cheetah.

Which animal talks the most?
A yakety-yak.

WHAT IS IT?

Angel Fish

Pig Sty (Pig's tie)

What do you call Eskimo cows?
Eskimoos.

Why is the letter F like a cow's tail?
Because it's at the end of beef.

What did one goat say to the other goat?
"Do you know where your kids are?"

What does a tiger do when it rains?
Gets wet.

Which has more legs, a lion or no lion?
No lion. A lion has four legs, but no lion has eight legs.

Why shouldn't you grab a lion's tail?
It may be only his tail, but it could be your end.

Two chimps, two seals, one elephant and a lion stood under one umbrella. Why didn't they get wet?
It wasn't raining.

What do you run into when it's raining cats and dogs?
Poodles.

What are the last three hairs on a dog's tail called?
Dog hairs.

What did the dog say when somebody cut its tail in half?
"It won't be long now."

Why do dogs chase their tails?
They're trying to make both ends meet.

Which dog keeps the best time?
A watchdog.

What do you get if you cross a watchdog with a werewolf?
A very nervous mailman.

What do you call a silly monkey?
A chumpanzee.

What does the government use when it takes a census of all the monkeys in the zoos?
An ape recorder.

Where did Noah keep the bees?
In archives.

What do bees do with all their honey?
Cell it.

What do you give a rhinoceros with big feet?
Large shoes.

What is black and white and red all over?
A sunburnt zebra.

What do you get if you cross a zebra with an ape man?
Tarzan stripes forever.

What do hippopotamuses have that no other animal has?
Baby hippopotamuses.

If there were ten cats in a boat and one jumped out, how many would be left?
None. They were all copycats.

What is the difference between a cat and a comma?
One has claws at the end of its paws, and the other a pause at the end of its clause.

What do you get if you cross an elephant with a kangaroo?
Great big holes all over Australia.

What do you get if you cross a mink with a kangaroo?
A fur coat with pockets.

What did the mother kangaroo say when she found the baby kangaroo was missing?
"Who picked my pocket?"

CAN YOU SAY IT?

Freddie Thrush flies through thick fog.

A clipper shipped several clipped sheep.
Were these clipped sheep the clipper
   ship's sheep?
Or just clipped sheep clipped by the
   clipper ship's clipper?

The rat ran by
the river with
a lump of raw
liver.

Three gray-green geese,
Feeding on a weedy piece.
The piece was weedy,
And the geese were greedy,
Three gray-green greedy geese.

· 10 ·
SEEING IS
BELIEVING

Here are some of the most difficult challenges in the book. Don't let your eyes deceive you. These puzzles are next to impossible. Good luck!

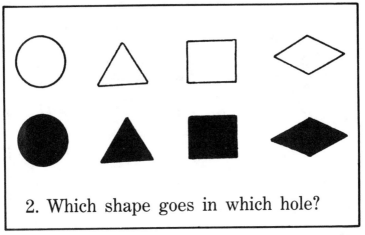

1. Which is the odd one out?

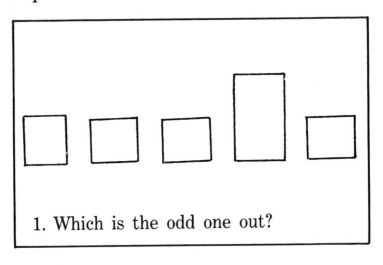

2. Which shape goes in which hole?

Answers on page 92.

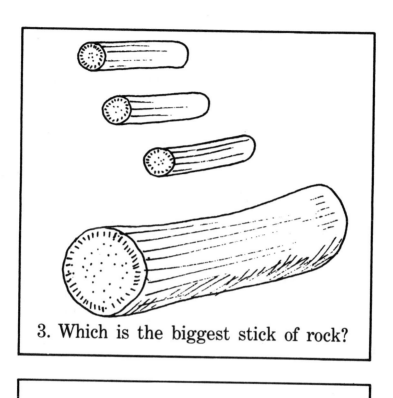

3. Which is the biggest stick of rock?

4. What is this drawing?

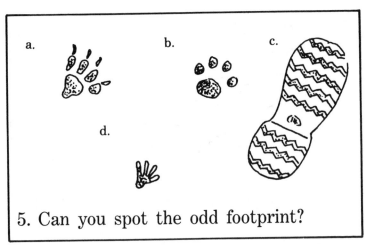

5. Can you spot the odd footprint?

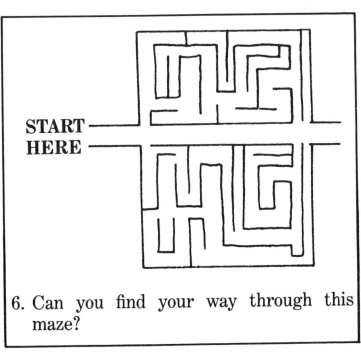

6. Can you find your way through this maze?

Answers on page 92.

Picture One

Picture Two

7. Can you spot twelve differences between these two pictures?

8. Only two of the clowns on this page are the same. Can you spot which two?

Answers on page 92.

9. Can you spot the odd one out of these?

10. Here are four owls. Can you spot which is the odd one out?

Answers

1. We think it's #1 and #4, but we're not sure. We had lots of trouble with this one.

2. What hole?

3. You think it's the one at the bottom, don't you? We did, too, but there isn't any rock. They're all logs.

4. A white cat in the snow.

5. They all look odd to us.

6. We couldn't get through it. We tried everything.

7. We could spot one difference. One of the hats is on an elephant.

8. No. They're all the same, aren't they?

9. The bunny on the right is sleeping.

10. Spot one owl and you've spotted them all.

· 11 ·
WEIRD &
WACKY

Answer: A Chinese frog.
Question: What sits on a lily and goes "Cloak, cloak"?

Answer: One is a hunted stag, the other a stunted hag.
Question: What is the difference between a deer being chased and a midget witch?

Answer: "Hello, hello, hello."
Question: What does a three-headed policeman say?

Answer: "I love you" ("I love ewe").
Question: What did the ram say to his girl friend?

Answer: Climate.
Question: If you could not go around a mountain, what would you do?

Answer: Zing.
Question: What do you do with a zong?

Answer: Zinc.
Question: Where do you wash your zaucepan?

Answer: Egg white.
Question: Name Snow White's brother.

Answer: Start from scratch.
Question: How can you tell if you've been bitten by a flea?

Answer: Ragtime.
Question: What time is it when your clothes wear out?

Answer: Laundress.
Question: What do you wear when you cut the grass?

Answer: Carpet.
Question: What is sold by the yard and worn by the foot?

Answer: Fission.
Question: What do scientists eat with chips?

Answer: Moonbeams.
Question: What holds the moon up?

Answer: Myth.
Question: What is a female moth?

Answer: Extinct.
Question: Describe a dead skunk.

· 12 ·
NO
LAUGHING
IN THE
LIBRARY

Who wrote *All About Kissing*?
        a. Maude D. Merrier
        b. Miss L. Toe
        c. Bella DeBall

Who put together that valuable
book *How to Get Rich Quick*?
        a. Robin Banks
        b. Jack Potts
        c. Kermit Grimes

Who wrote that useful book
How to Avoid Arguments?
        a. Xavier Breath
        b. Howard I. No
        c. Thayer Thorry

Which athlete wrote the best seller called
Keeping Fit?
        a. Lena Body
        b. Ivor Blister
        c. Carrie Mae Holm

We all love ghost stories, but do you know who wrote *This House Is Haunted?*
    a. Les Greta Way
    b. Hugo First
    c. Gladys Daylight

Who wrote *Everybody's Guide to Wild Animals?*
    a. Bab Boone
    b. Ann T. Lope
    c. Claudia Armoff

Who wrote *Can You Solve My Problem?*
  a. Dan Druff
  b. Phil McAvity
  c. Fred I. Kant

Who wrote *I Am Hopelessly Lost?*
  a. R. U. Shore
  b. Wes D. Eggzit
  c. Wareham I. Now

A love story called *Is This Love?* was penned by:
  a. Nedda Chance
  b. Tamara Knight
  c. Midas Welby

No answers will be found on page 128.

Fiction Best-Seller List

1. *To Market, to Market* by Tobias A. Pigg

2. *Peekaboo!* by I.C. Hugh

3. *The Drunkards* by Carrie M. Home

4. *Banbury Cross* by Rhoda Whitehorse

5. *Knock Out* by I.C. Stozz

6. *Japanese Weekend* by Sat Sun Mon

7. *Out on Bail* by Frieda Convict

8. *Early to Bed* by R. U. Upjohn

Non-Fiction Best-Seller List

1. *How Things Get Lost* by Lucy Lastic

2. *The Empty Tank* by Phil R. Upp

3. *Fitting Carpets* by Walter Wall

4. *End of the Week* by Gladys Friday

5. *My Life in the Lunatic Asylum* by I. M. Knotts

6. *Insomnia* by Eliza Wake

7. *How to Improve Your Target Shooting* by Mister Completely

8. *Why You Need Insurance* by Justin Case

WHO SAID IT?

"Let's make the King a big scrambled egg."
All the King's Men who couldn't put Humpty Dumpty back together again.

"2B or not 2B, that is the question."
The absentminded professor who couldn't remember which class he was supposed to teach.

"Will you please join me?"
A person who was coming apart.

"You can't pin anything on me."
A nudist to the D.A.

"Dr. Livingstone, I Presume."
Mr. Presume, introducing himself to Dr. Livingstone.

What did the book say to the librarian?
"May I take you out?"

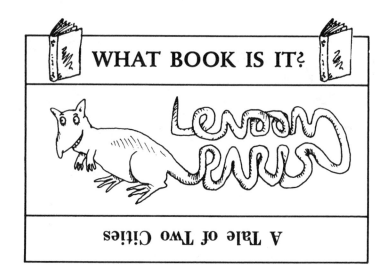

WHAT BOOK IS IT?

A Tale of Two Cities

· 13 ·
RIDDLE-IC-ULOUS!

What is worse than raining cats and dogs?
Hailing buses.

What did the dirt say to the rain?
"If this keeps up, my name will be mud."

Why was the letter damp?
Because there was postage dew.

What is the noisiest season?
A rusty spring.

What is the difference between an umbrella and someone who never stops talking?
You can shut up an umbrella.

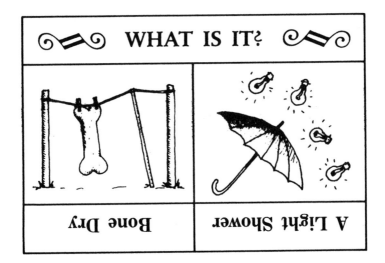

WHAT IS IT?

Bone Dry

A Light Shower

What keys never open locked doors?
Monkeys.

How do you make anti-freeze?
Hide her nightie.

What is black and white and black and
white and black and white?
*A nun rolling down a snowbank with a
penguin under her arm.*

If you had twenty cows and a man gave
you thirty cows, what would you have?
A dairy farm.

Did you hear about the little kid who wanted to buy a parrot?

He didn't have enough money, so he bought a bird that was going cheap.

CHEEP!

How do you stop fish from smelling?

Hold their noses.

What happened when the sardine was late to work?

He got canned.

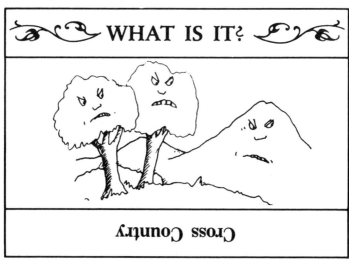

WHAT IS IT?

Cross Country

Why did the rich lady buy a Ming vase?
To go with her Ming coat.

What is the best way to make a pair of trousers last?
Make the jacket first.

If you found a ten-dollar bill in every pocket of your jacket, what would you have?
Someone else's jacket.

Why are a star and an old barn on a farmyard exactly the same?
They both contain R-A-T-S.

Did you hear about the dog that ate nothing but garlic?

His bark was worse than his bite.

I thought a thought. But the thought I thought wasn't the thought I thought I thought. If the thought I thought I thought had been the thought I thought, I wouldn't have thought so much.

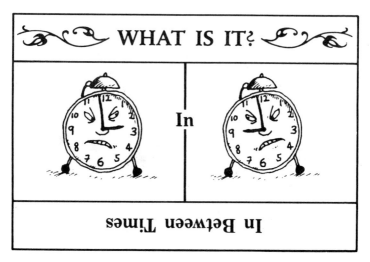

· 14 ·
BRAIN POWER

It is in the center of gravity and always invaluable. It is out of tune, but the first to be vocal. It is invisible, though clearly seen in the middle of a river. Three join it in vice and three are in love with it. In vain you will look for it, for it has been in heaven a long time, and now lies in the grave. What is it?
The letter V.

What goes from New York to Philadelphia without moving?
The road.

What is the difference between a glass of soda and a glass of water?
About 40¢.

What gets wetter the more it dries?
A towel.

If a girl falls down a hole why can't her brother help her out?

Because he can't be a brother and assist her (a sister) too.

How can you take two letters away from a four-letter word and have four left?

Take F and E from FIVE and leave IV.

WHAT IS IT?

Spy Ring

What is French for idiot?

Lagoon.

Where was Solomon's temple?

At the side of Solomon's head.

Why is it so hard to get a minute to ourselves?
Because the minutes are not hours (ours).

What did the coin say when it got stuck in the parking meter?
"Money's tight these days."

What is the U.S. national flower?
The cost-of-living rose.

Which snake is good at counting money?
An adder.

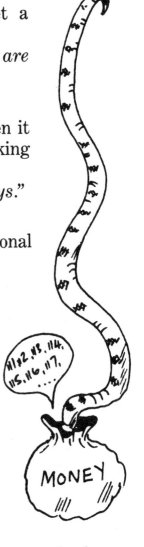

How are money and secrets alike?
They are both hard to keep.

Why couldn't the church steeple keep a secret?
Because the bell always tolled.

What increases in value when it is turned upside down?
The number 6.

A man needed a new set of teeth and went along to a new shop in town that had rows and rows of dentures in the window. He was just deciding which set to get when a policeman came along and arrested him. What for?
For picking his teeth in public.

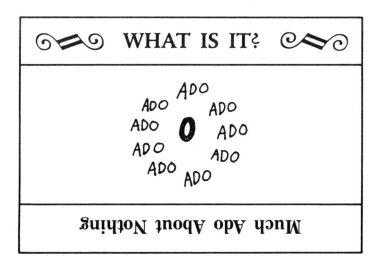

WHAT IS IT?

Much Ado About Nothing

Which word of six letters means exactly the opposite if you change the places of the middle two letters?
United and untied.

WHO SAID IT?

"Ah, it all comes back to me now."
A skunk, when the wind changed direction.

"You light up my life."
The ceiling to the chandelier.

"Ho, ho, ho, plop!"
Santa Claus laughing his head off.

"I see your drawers."
The carpet to the desk.

"Look at the orange marmalade."
The chicken when the mother hen laid an orange.

· 15 ·
WRAPPING
IT UP

Did you hear about
the girl who goes
out with the
violinist?
*He strings her
along.*

Did you hear about the man who cleans his
own chimney?
Now there's a guy who soots himself!

Did you hear about the kleptomaniac's
daughter?
She takes after her mother.

Did you hear about
the elevator
operator?
*He has his ups
and downs.*

What did one
elevator say to the
other elevator?
*"I think I'm
coming down with
something."*

When is the sea friendliest?
When it waves.

What is brown,
hairy and wears
sunglasses?
*A coconut on
vacation.*

Who is strong enough to hold up a car with
one hand?
A traffic cop.

Who can shave four times a day and still
have a beard?
A barber.

What did one weasel say to the other
weasel?
"My pop is bigger than your pop."

What did the laundryman say to the very
impatient customer?
"Keep your shirt on!"

What goes out black and comes in white?
A black dog on a snowy day.

What did the cannibal say when he saw three hunters driving up in a jeep?
"Ah—meals on wheels!"

What do you say to Emillion when he does you a good turn?
"Thanks, Emillion!"

What did Cinderella say when her photographs did not arrive?
"Some day my prints will come."

Where do frogs fly flags?
On tadpoles.

What always succeeds?
A toothless parakeet.

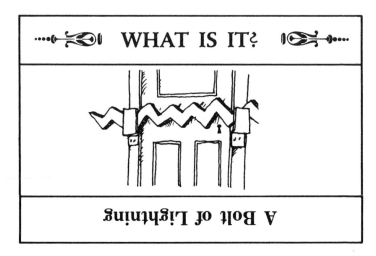

WHAT IS IT?

A Bolt of Lightning

Why do demons and ghouls get on so well?
Because demons are a ghoul's best friend.

What is a ghost's favorite jewel?
A tombstone.

What do ghosts eat for breakfast?
Dreaded (shredded) wheat.

What do ghosts put on hot turkey sandwiches?
Grave-y.

When is it unlucky to have a black cat cross your path?
When you are a mouse.

What do you call a 7-foot tall, 300-pound Sylvester Stallone look-alike with his portable radio going full blast?
Anything you want—he won't hear you.

Where is the best place to weigh whales?
At a whale-weigh station.

Why was the farmer cross?
Because someone stepped on his corn.

How can you always find a liar out?
Go to his house when he isn't in.

What kind of cat has 8 feet?
An octopus.

What happened when the cat swallowed a penny?
There was some money in the kitty.

What do you get when you feed lemons to a cat?
A sourpuss.

WHAT IS IT?

Sleeping Bag

If an egg floated down the River Nile, where would it have come from?
A chicken.

Why was the fisherman arrested?
Because he carried a rod.

Why did the rabbit sleep in the salad dressing?
So it could get up oily in the morning.

What happened to the man who hit himself on the head with an axe?
He got a splitting headache.

Why did the germ cross the microscope?
To get to the other slide.

Did you hear about the couple who met in the revolving door?
They stopped going around together.

What is the difference between a chocolate chip cookie and an elephant?
You can't dunk an elephant in your milk.

What do you get if you cross a quarterback and an elephant?
I don't know, but if it wants to score a touchdown, don't try to stop it.

CAN YOU SAY IT?

Five French friars fanning a fainted flea.

Greek grapes grow graciously.

A truly rural frugal ruler's mural.

She stops at the shops where I shop, and if she stops at the shops where I shop, I won't stop at the shops where she shops.

Lesser leather never weathered lesser wetter weather.

WHAT ARE THESE PICTURES?

T   I   STITCH   M   E

A Stitch in Time

Funny Bone

Witchcraft

FRIEND STANDING FRIEND
mis

A little misunderstanding between friends.